W9-CXZ-613

The
Saint Nicholas
Secret

A heartwarming story of faith lost and hope regained.

As a child, Dennis Engleman's first, sad experience of losing faith in Santa Claus had long-lasting effects. But then, on a business trip, he discovered the truth about his childhood hero.

"Ironically, I regained my belief in St. Nicholas
just as my children were on the verge of losing theirs."

After he finds out St. Nicholas' secret, the author is able to transfer his own children's affections from the "sweet myth of Santa Claus" to a dynamic faith in St. Nicholas

The Saint Nichcolas Secret is for every grown-up child who mourns his lost miracles, and every parent who wants to save her children from that same heartbreak.

The

Saint Nicholas Secret

A Story of Childhood Faith
Reborn in the Heart of a Father

by Dennis E. Engleman

Conciliar Press
Ben Lomond, California

The Saint Nicholas Secret
© Copyright 1999 by Dennis E. Engleman

All Rights Reserved

Published by   Conciliar Press
                 P.O. Box 76
                 Ben Lomond, California 95005-0076

Printed in the United States of America

ISBN 1-888212-15-2

To my dear mother
Who taught me to pray . . .
And to hope in St. Nicholas

Table of Contents

About This Book

Children of many cultures learn early to believe in Santa Claus. To them he is both virtually omniscient, knowing of their good or bad behavior, and virtually omnipotent, capable of the stupendous feats of flying and visiting homes throughout the world on Christmas night. While fictional characters such as Peter Pan and Superman remain in the backwaters of fantasy and are not expected actually to appear in one's living room, Santa Claus is confidently supposed to tumble down chimneys, leave presents, then feast on milk and cookies.

Television, film, books, and (most significantly) parents persuade youngsters that this eccentric and amazing personage is actually real—that he can and will influence their young lives. When such an authoritative cultural message is reinforced by the receipt of delightful gifts, children are only too glad to believe in the benevolent man in red.

This situation provides the context for one of childhood's earliest conflicts of faith. After a while, children begin to suspect something is wrong with the stereotypical Santa Claus of shopping malls. As maturity refines their sense of the credible, his exploits begin to strain reasonable credulity. When these forlorn suspicions are finally confirmed by the very adults who had formerly fostered their faith in Santa Claus as an imaginary being, many children experience some degree of emotional and spiritual trauma.

It is a sad moment when these children suffer not only the loss of their beloved Christmas benefactor, but also the awareness of having been deceived by those in whom they should have had most reason to trust. It is no use then to speak of "good intentions" or to suggest that such painful experiences are justified merely by being commonplace. Innocent hearts cannot easily comprehend why the Santa Claus who had previously been touted so highly is suddenly gone forever, and in fact never really existed. Even when their immediate sorrow and anger have passed, a sense of betrayal may linger, perhaps only dimly perceived, for years to come.

Yet to deny children this Christmas tradition would be unkind, if not impossible. In spite of Santa's logic-defying escapades and the commercial abuses to which his name and image are subjected, generations have rightly perceived him to be both boon and blessing. The incongruity lies not in his saintly character, but rather in a worldly culture so impervious to spirituality and insensible of the truly miraculous that it presents Santa as a farce and a cartoon, eventual disbelief in whom is inescapable.

But how is one to teach this delightful tradition to children and still preserve them from later disappointment? There is a way, a simple yet profound way—which we may call the St. Nicholas Secret. It is revealed in this volume, which is a mostly true story both for adults and for the children who will one day be adults. It is the story of how one child's broken faith eventually led, through strange twists, to his grown-up renewal of faith. And it is the story of St. Nicholas, that mysterious, otherworldly, and absolutely real person who has one foot on the rooftop and the other in eternity.

1

∞

A Christmas Prayer

"What would you like St. Nicholas to give you for Christmas?" Mother smiled while putting the immense question to me.

"'Can I have whatever I want?" I asked, trying to fathom a choice of this magnitude.

"'If you are a good boy," she replied, then returned to ironing clothes.

But was I a good boy? A sticky question indeed! My recent past offered good grounds for worry. I recalled a broken flowerpot, one of Mother's favorite Florida vacation mementos (she was always partial to flaming pink flamingoes). And what about the day I hid under the kitchen sink when Mother was trying to find me? Santa must surely have heard of that, since she was rather upset! Then there were things I wasn't sure counted, like getting toys stuck in the toilet.

Overwhelmed with the memory of these disasters, for so they seemed to my young mind, I might have done nothing to solicit Santa's good will. But Mother made a suggestion which marked a turning point in my life.

"Why don't you send Santa a letter?" she said. "I'll help you."

And so I dictated a note which she wrote on a yellow sheet of paper with a fat lead pencil. It read:

> Dear St. Nicholas,
>   Please bring me something nice.
> I have tried to be good. I love you.
>   Your friend,
>   Dennis Engleman

The possibility of communicating directly with St. Nicholas was a revelation to me. Especially since, when Christmas morning dawned, something nice was indeed under the tree. This proved he had gotten my message!

But where had Mother sent the letter? The North Pole, she said. And so every year after this, I wrote to St. Nicholas religiously. As December's frigid breezes made the brown leaves swirl, I struggled to compose messages expressing my affection and hopes, addressed them to the North Pole, and deposited them carefully in the mailbox down the street.

I supposed that St. Nicholas lived at the North Pole in a cozy little house surmounted by blankets of snow. I imagined his elves camped in little igloos on his front lawn, rows and rows of them, like the neatly ordered tents of an army bivouac. Santa's sleigh, of course, was parked next to his stone fireplace so he could exit his house the same way he would enter mine. His reindeer scampered outside in the white snowdrifts, eagerly awaiting their annual time-defying flight across the globe. In the meantime they played mischievous games with Rudolph's nose and occasionally tripped over the elves' igloos, which always created a great ruckus.

For me it was one of life's truths that Santa and his elves, in their quaint workshop, could build enough toys in a year's time to give every good child on earth one or two. Nor was it any trouble to believe that he could fit millions of gifts into his bag and deliver them all over the world via airborne sled in a single night, Christmas Eve. Santa's omniscience in knowing what each person deserved was as credible as the proposition that this rotund old man could slide down the narrowest of chimneys unscathed—including those that led to gas furnaces!

St. Nicholas was better than presidents or kings, singing idols

᠅ *A Christmas Prayer*

or sports heroes. He was better than comic book titans. Spiderman, Batman, and Superman might conjure a fantastic world, but in the end it was only fiction. Peter Pan and the Wizard of Oz had their moments, but Santa was forever.

I loved him, I hoped in him, I believed in him. But St. Nicholas was nevertheless a baffling and mysterious character. How did he do what he did? Why did he do it? What was his Secret?

2

A Closing Door

St. Nicholas convinced me that miracles were a natural part of life, something one had every reason to expect and depend on. If he could fly, never grow older, bestow wonderful gifts, and do everything else that he obviously did, then *anything* was possible! His very existence meant the universe was a benevolent place in which all kinds of good things could, and most likely would, occur.

But as the years passed, the "miraculous" became increasingly harder to accept. Santa's cheery red cheeks beckoned from cardboard pictures in store windows surrounded by tinseled merchandise, but the illogical logistics of his escapades began to raise troubling questions. How could he make so many toys? How could he get them all in his bag? How did he know where someone lived after he or she had moved to a new home? What kept his sleigh in the air without wings?

Nor were these questions made less perplexing by finding "Santa" in mall after mall, listening with vacant eyes and stiff knees to hordes of bellowing children. How did he leave one place where we had just shopped in time to beat us to the next? Why did he look so thin? Why were his eyebrows black instead of white? Why did his beard seem to be falling off?

At first only faint, fearful suspicions, my doubts grew. I wanted to believe, but needed help. Finally I summoned the courage to lay the terrible question to rest.

"Mother, is there really a St. Nicholas?" I asked one night, trembling.

She glanced up from a sink full of dishes with a strange look on her face. Maybe she felt regret—or maybe relief—but she only shrugged her shoulders and said simply, "No, there isn't."

Mother did not explain how there could be no St. Nicholas when I had been told so many times that he was real. She did not say why I had been taught to believe in something that could be snatched away with a word. She did not offer any justification for the disappointment I felt, the sense of loss so casually inflicted—or so it seemed to me. Perhaps Mother had forgotten what it was to believe in something grand. Perhaps she had never known, since her life had been hard.

Finally, after I had stared sightlessly at the yellow and green patterns on the linoleum floor for a long time, Mother said, "Now you are older. Now you can understand more. You don't need to believe in miracles."

After that I went to my room and quietly closed the door. I had an empty feeling inside, for a door in my heart was also quietly closing—a door to the chamber of childhood dreams, where hope and faith are nurtured in the light of trust. And after that I could not keep hoping and believing, for a world without miracles was a world without anything to hope for or to believe in.

The Christmas presents under the tree that year seemed ordinary, for I knew elfin hands had not fashioned them. Nor had they been delivered wondrously, but rather purchased from noisy stores. The colored lights and bright decorations which had formerly intimated the impending arrival of a mysterious and hugely loving presence now gleamed in tawdry hypocrisy.

After this, everyday events took on a monotonous quality. Weeks and years passed in that flat sameness which characterizes so much of human existence. Nothing out of the ordinary seemed possible. My youth revolved around a tedious sequence of inconsequential events, few of which can be conjured now into memory, fewer still with pleasure. The inane seasons of growing up flashed past my awareness like a grade B movie. All the world had to offer, apparently, was trivial entertainments and pointless pursuits. Life was boring.

3

The Miracle of Faith

Eventually I married my sweetheart and we had three children of our own. Once our kids grew old enough to understand that Christmas was a special time, I resolved to do everything possible to spare John, Lily, and Victoria the disappointment which I had suffered about St. Nicholas.

Consequently, I never spoke of the "man in red." I did not

recite *The Night Before Christmas* or lead my children to expect the magical appearance of gifts. We did not listen for reindeer hooves on the roof. We did not put out milk and cookies. We did not write letters to the North Pole.

Instead, we avoided television and quietly read stories about the Three Wise Men and Good King Wenceslas. We made decorations of oranges stuck with cloves and sang old-fashioned carols. We gathered pine cones and sprinkled them with glitter. Most of all, we talked about Baby Jesus and His Mother, Mary.

Yet even these precautions were not enough, for one morning I overheard the following conversation:

"What do you want St. Nicholas to bring you, Lily?" John whispered to his little sister.

"A doll, but I don't know if his elves make the kind I like," she replied earnestly.

"They can make any kind," John affirmed. "They make all the toys for the whole world at the North Pole."

A thoughtful silence followed, and at last Lily continued, "But how does Santa fly over the ocean and find everyone's house at night?"

"He has radar," replied her brother authoritatively. "And besides, Rudolph's nose is very bright!"

My surreptitious, house-robed presence was revealed at that moment by an inauspicious sneeze. "Papa," Lily clamored, spotting me. "John says St. Nicholas has radar in his sleigh! Is that true?"

The conversation I had taken such pains to avoid was imminent.

"Radar!" I replied, wondering how to sidestep the inquiry.

"Yes, and he says Rudolph's nose is bright enough to see our house even through the clouds!"

"Well, that could explain why airplanes never report flying into reindeer," I said anxiously. John looked pleased and marched off in triumph.

So in spite of parental blockades, St. Nicholas had already climbed down the chimney and taken up residence in our home! Does it always happen this way, I wondered? Does he always kindle childhood faith sort of . . . miraculously?

In the eager faces of John, Lily, and Victoria, a familiar hope and faith glowed that had nothing to do with wanting gifts. The doors to their chambers of childhood dreams stood wide open, allowing the gentle light of trust to shine forth. Like the gleam of stars penetrating infinite space, that light spanned the furthest reaches of cosmic goodness, assuring them of love even in the midst of a vast eternity.

4

Troubling Questions

Predictably, it wasn't much longer before John, the oldest, began to apply critical reasoning to Santa's yearly feat. "How can St. Nicholas put all the presents for the children of the world into his bag?" he asked, more curious than suspicious.

"That would have to be a very large bag, wouldn't it?" I replied noncommittally.

"Yes." But then he brightened. "My best friend Andrew thinks that Santa shrinks the toys so they fit into his bag, and when he puts them under the Christmas tree they grow to regular size again."

Sister Lily had a simpler theory. "I think the presents just somehow come down from heaven by themselves," she said, regarding further detail as unnecessary. Fortunately, little Victoria was too small to inquire into the subject.

These questions troubled me, for I knew it was only a matter of time before they asked *the* question. I dreaded the thought of repeating that conversation which my mother and I had shared so long ago, and was not sure I could make a better job of it than she had.

Innocent hearts can believe and be saved or be broken and lost.

Children naturally entertain various immature notions about reality; in the normal course of time many such ideas fall away without consequence. But if the subject touches on life's essential nature, meaning, or purpose, disillusionment can be devastating.

Faith requires the miraculous. Eventually my children would notice, as I had done, that "the man in red" sat in every shopping mall and didn't really *know* them. They would sense that this super consumer curiosity was no wonder-worker, but rather a tacky fraud. Unwillingly, reluctantly, they would start to disbelieve.

This first, sad experience of losing faith can have effects that last a lifetime, as I knew well. I hated to think of John, Lily, and Victoria repeating the sad experiences of my own childhood. But what could be done?

5

The Scent of Sanctity

Being an electrical engineer by trade, I was occasionally obliged to troubleshoot recalcitrant industrial machines in distant locations. About this time my company arranged for me to visit several customers in Europe. Stops were scheduled around Paris, then on into Italy—Rome, Florence, and Bari. Work went rather smoothly in France, and I found myself near Chartres with a little time on my hands. I used this opportunity to visit the twelfth-century cathedral for which that town is world-renowned.

Chartres Cathedral is an amazing sight, decorated with thousands of stone carvings depicting Christianity's teachings. I joined a crowd which had gathered for a tour of the statuary and stained-glass windows. A little white-haired man was serving as guide, his pale features suggesting a life spent within the great church's deep blue shadows. The guide drew our attention to a stone carving above a set of magnificent doors.

"Around sixteen hundred years ago," he said, "a Christian couple named Theophanes and Nonna lived in the town of Patara in Asia Minor. They were rich, but sad, for they had no children. Nevertheless, they trusted God, and tried to live righteously. They were very generous with their wealth, giving liberally to the poor. By many acts of mercy, together with tears and fervent prayers, they begged God to give them a child. At last, when they were very old, the Lord blessed these faithful and pious servants with a son, whom they named Nicholas—which means in Greek, 'Victor.' "

"The only St. Nicholas I know of is the fairy-tale guy who wears a red suit," I commented wryly to a person at my side.

The guide overheard my remark. "This St. Nicholas is the very one upon whom the Santa Claus legend is based," he informed the crowd.

"You mean there was a real St. Nicholas?" I asked in astonishment.

"Yes, he lived in the fourth century," the guide replied curtly,

Sculpture of St. Nicholas, Chartres Cathedral.

The Saint Nicholas Secret ☙

then turned back to the others. "Nicholas' virtue came from his love of God. He was an ardent Christian, accustomed to long vigils of prayer in the dead of night. He was ordained to the priesthood at an early age, and tried to imitate the angels through fasting, ceaseless prayer, and acts of selfless service. Nicholas considered his true home to be in heaven, for Christ had said, 'My kingdom is not of this world.' As a result of his otherworldly focus, he was extraordinarily generous with earthly possessions. Following the death of his parents he gave away his inheritance, and many stories are recorded of his acts of charity."

The guide pointed to the lower right portion of the sculpture, in which a man was lying in bed. Around him stood three young girls expressing grief and despair. Enclosing this group was a wall, and outside it stood another man who was thrusting a bag through a hole in the wall toward the sorrowing family.

"Here is a depiction of one of St. Nicholas' most well-known acts of mercy," he continued. "This prostrate father was too poor to give his three daughters a dowry, so they had no chance of being married. God revealed the man's dilemma to the priest Nicholas, who then secretly tossed a sack of gold into his house at midnight. At the sight of this great gift, the man wept for joy and thanked God, for his oldest daughter was then able to marry. Nicholas noted the man's righteous behavior, and returned a second time by night with another sack of gold. The second daughter was then also able to marry. At this, however, the father begged God to reveal his secret benefactor. He did not sleep for many nights, patiently waiting beneath the window of his home. Finally he was rewarded, for St. Nicholas quietly approached, tossed a sack of gold through the window, and hurried away. The man ran after the servant of God and fell at his feet, kissing them with thanksgiving."

"Why didn't St. Nicholas just give the gold outright?" someone in the crowd asked.

"Nicholas wished to help the family, but the Gospel of Matthew says: 'Take heed that ye do not your alms before men,' " the guide explained. "Nicholas did not want to draw attention or praise to himself. He wanted to receive the favor of God alone. Still, his generous nature has endeared him to posterity. He is today memorialized the world over as a secret giver. Just recall the Santa Claus tale: Does not St. Nicholas sneak into the house while everyone is asleep, leave gifts which he has brought in a bag, and depart unseen?"

"He must have been a very popular person, even in his life-time," another visitor commented.

"Actually, the saint's greatest desire was to stay in the isolation and seclusion of a monastery," the guide said. "When Nicholas reached Jerusalem, he hoped to remain there as a monk, devoting himself to silence and contemplation of God. But Christ did not wish the saint's light to be hidden from mankind. While standing in prayer, Nicholas heard a voice from God telling him to go back into the world and serve Him there. So Nicholas went to the city of Myra, where no one knew him. He remained in the church day and night, engrossed in prayer.

"At that time the bishop of Myra died. Consequently all the

bishops of the area gathered to choose a new bishop for the city, praying that God Himself would reveal His choice in this matter. An angel appeared, commanding the bishops to go to the church during the night and observe all who came. Whoever should be first to enter, said the angel, would be God's choice for bishop of Myra, and that man's name would be Nicholas. Accordingly, the bishops stood that night where the angel had directed, and waited. As the time for the morning service approached, Nicholas hastened to the church, for his habit was to arise at midnight and arrive before others."

"So St. Nicholas did not want to be bishop?" someone asked. "He just happened to like going to church very early and because of that he was chosen?"

"Yes. He tried to refuse the appointment, but finally submitted to God's will. As bishop, Nicholas was meek and forgiving to others while bold in defense of Christianity. He wore simple clothing and ate only once a day. He spent his time in prayer or in service. To orphans he was a father, to the poor a merciful giver, to the weeping a comforter, to the wronged a helper, and to all a great benefactor. He zealously destroyed pagan temples, and the evil spirits which inhabited them ran away in terror."

"But all this is pious legend, right?" I broke in anxiously. "There is no proof St. Nicholas did any of these things?"

"We do not call it legend, my friend, but rather Holy Tradition," the guide insisted. "And on the contrary, there is abundance of proof. St. Nicholas did many things—even miracles—

which are documented in the courts of Byzantine emperors."

"Miracles?" I said the word slowly, as though it were an incantation.

"Yes, indeed. Once Nicholas made a pilgrimage to Palestine in order to venerate the holy places of our Lord's life. As his ship sailed near Egypt, he warned the sailors that a storm would arise. Unexpectedly, the heavens began to blow and the sea heaved wildly. Soon the ship was breaking apart, and the sailors entreated St. Nicholas to save them. He commanded them to have faith in God and knelt in fervent prayer. Immediately the sea became peaceful, and the sailors were doubly astonished—both at their passenger's foretelling of the storm and at its cessation. Nor was this the only time the saint rescued those in trouble. Seafarers caught in other storms

Icon of St. Nicholas saving the mariners.

The Saint Nicholas Secret ॐ

often testified that, at their prayers, he calmed the seas and pre-served them from death. He also appeared in dreams to emperors and prisoners alike, in order to save those who were unjustly condemned."

I felt a lump growing in my throat and tried to dispel it with objections. "But it was easier for people to have faith way back then," I protested. "Even ordinary things seemed miraculous. Now we can understand more! We don't need to believe in miracles!"

My voice echoed oddly through the soaring vaults. It reverberated among flapping pigeons and returned to my ears strange yet familiar, crying words which had sat like millstones on my heart since they were first uttered to me: *Now you are older. Now you can understand more. You don't need to believe in miracles.*

I looked about at the staring eyes like one caught in a criminal act. I wondered if my face might be bright red—or ghostly white. I thought of running away, or perhaps collapsing and feigning death. My mind was wrestling with crazy possibilities when the guide's soft voice stopped it abruptly.

"We still need to believe in miracles, but we have forgotten how," he said quietly. "Or we think they are weak little things which cannot exist without our puny faith. But look up here, what do you see?"

He pointed to the scene in the sculpture above that of the poor father with his three daughters. Here St. Nicholas himself was lying prone, dressed as a bishop, evidently dead. Below his casket were a number of people with jars and bottles.

"It looks like people are trying to revive him with medicines," someone suggested.

"But the truth is just the opposite," the guide replied. "St. Nicholas' earthly life ended on December 6, 343. We celebrate December 6 as his feast day—rather than his worldly birthday—because it was on this day that he was, as it were, born into heaven. And to confirm to all generations that the saint *does* reside in heaven, God permitted a special wonder to take place. St. Nicholas' bones began to produce a fragrant liquid. First only drops, then more and more gushed forth until the entire sarcophagus was filled to overflowing. This sweet-smelling oil had great healing powers, and people from all over the world came to his tomb to collect it in jars."

The idea struck me as repugnant. "Something oozed out of his skeleton?"

"When a saint's body is sanctified through total surrender to Christ, then even his bones are no more of this world," the guide replied. "They are sacred conveyors of God's mercy. If you look closely at the sculpture, you will see holes in the stone coffin through which this precious fluid is flowing out. Beneath this are believers who have gathered to catch it in bottles or allow it to drip onto them."

"Maybe some mold had gathered in the dampness of the crypt," I suggested. "There is bound to be a scientific explanation for this."

The guide smiled patiently. "Imagine, if you will," he said, "the finest perfume in the world, made by painstaking processes from rare and delicate flowers. Even a drop of this exquisite scent fills the room with lovely fragrances too subtle to describe. Such was the Holy Myrrh coming from St. Nicholas, for so it was called since there was no better way to describe the heavenly substance. The Holy Myrrh affected the physical senses in a most uplifting way. But that is not all; the spiritual faculties benefited even more. Those who were sick of bodily or mental diseases had only to apply the Holy Myrrh to obtain healing. And to all, its otherworldly fragrance imparted a sweet perception of that heavenly realm from which St. Nicholas continues to bestow blessings."

"But surely *this* is pious legend!" I cried in agitation. "What proof is there that this . . . this Holy Myrrh has helped anyone?"

"In the Greek village of Sparta lived a peasant named Doulos, whose daughter Kyriakula was blind," the guide said. "Every tenth of May, all the people of that region would gather at the local Orthodox monastery to venerate a wonder-working icon of St. Nicholas. Doulos had taken Kyriakula to many doctors without obtaining her healing, and decided at last to bring her to St. Nicholas. For two days and nights, father and daughter supplicated the saint while Kyriakula's eyes were anointed with Holy Myrrh. Suddenly, on the third day at dawn, Kyriakula stood and crossed herself. 'Father, I see!' she cried. 'There are the saint's candles! There is the icon!' "

"And when did this happen?" I asked, frowning.

"In the eighteenth century," the guide replied.

"But St. Nicholas died in the fourth century! Do you mean

Holy Myrrh could be found fourteen hundred years after that?"

"There is Holy Myrrh even now," the guide answered serenely. "It has never stopped flowing from the saint's relics."

I stared at his pale face in bewilderment. Most fanciful legends have their basis in such a distant past they can be neither proved nor disproved. But this story was beginning to sound more and more real. Still, I resisted.

"It's impossible." I shook my head. "How could something from a dead man's bones far away in Myra—that's in Asia Minor, right?— how could this myrrh stuff heal anyone?"

"It is St. Nicholas himself who works the wonders by the power of God, my friend. The Holy Myrrh serves to increase one's faith, you see, so the miracle can come more easily." He paused and smiled slightly. "And the saint's tomb is no longer in Myra—it is now in Bari, Italy."

6

A Holy Embrace

I traveled on to Rome and Florence, and as in France, my duties were accomplished without difficulty. It seemed a strange coincidence that this business trip included Bari, the very city where St. Nicholas—as I now knew—was buried. Once in Bari, I decided to explore the ancient walled Byzantine village at the heart of the modern city.

How St. Nicholas' bones had reached Bari from Myra in Asia Minor was another mystery soon to be solved. I discovered that in the year 1087 a flotilla of Italians bent on possessing the saint's remains (called "relics") sailed to Myra and brought them back to Italy. This great effort, called the "Translation," reveals how important St. Nicholas was to the Christian world even seven hundred years after his death. The Italians wanted the constantly flowing Holy Myrrh, of course. But more than that, they wanted the blessings and healings associated with this great miracle-worker.

Passing under arches surmounted by icons, I followed convoluted alleys in which noisy children played ball. The streets were so narrow that in places my outstretched arms could almost touch the open doorways of the homes to either side. In the subdued afternoon light I caught a glimpse of a tall, white bell tower. After many curves and turns I reached an open courtyard which was dominated by a magnificent old church. "Basilica Pontifica Di S. Nicola," read a sign on the door.

Entering the ancient structure, I paused to feel the effect of centuries of worship. Massive wooden beams intersected with grey stone walls, creating an impression of prayerful strength. This was no tourist attraction; I was alone within the great edifice. Moving through silence, I walked all around the church. Near the altar were stairs leading downward. They descended into gloom; I traversed them warily, half expecting a macabre sight suddenly to accost my vision.

At the bottom of the stairs was a heavy wooden door. I pushed cautiously and it moved aside, revealing a small room beneath the

St. Nicholas Basilica, Bari, Italy. Crypt and sarcophagus.

The Saint Nicholas Secret ॐ

main altar—the crypt. Here, tapers were burning from candleholders attached to stone pillars and wooden beams. A few dark benches, now empty, invited visitors to rest and pray. Beyond them was a stone sarcophagus, bathed in the faint light of candles. Above it, an icon of St. Nicholas appeared to survey me compassionately. A sense of holiness and expectant waiting hung in the air.

Soon the fatigue of travel evaporated and I found myself remembering friends and family members. Without effort, or even realizing how it started, I began praying for people—particularly children. And strangest of all, I felt that someone was *listening* to my prayers. Even coaxing, as though to say, "Yes, go on! And what about so-and-so?"

Many an old acquaintance came to mind and I reflected on his or her special need, always with the distinct impression that this invisible someone was, as it were, taking notes. Eventually I perceived a kind of question being directed at me from the presence which had listened so intently to my prayers. It was not audible, but seemed to ask: "And you . . . what do you desire?"

At this, my eyes stung and I was overcome with a sense of grief and loss. How long had it been since I believed in miraculous gifts from above? "Can I have whatever I want?" I thought.

For I did desire something. Something unique and hard to find. Something a little boy had lost a long time ago and had never forgotten. But that thing was big and would probably never fit in St. Nicholas' bag. So I just repeated my simple childhood prayer:

Dear St. Nicholas,

    Please bring me something nice.
I have tried to be good. I love you.

        Your friend,

        Dennis Engleman

Then I felt a warm wetness on my cheeks and realized that tears were flowing. They dripped to the cold stone floor, and with them seemed to flow away years of sadness. My heart felt like a sink whose stopper is suddenly removed. A pool of betrayed faith and devastated hope drained away, leaving behind only quiet emptiness.

At last I opened my moist eyes and saw a Vespers prayer to St. Nicholas which lay on the nearby reading stand. It read:

A Holy Embrace

Thou O Nicholas the wise hast shone forth on earth by the rays of thy miracles. . . . O Saint Nicholas, the glorious, thou holy preacher of Christ, thou art a great and warm protector of those in danger: both on earth and sailing the seas whether they be far or near, for thou art a most compassionate and mighty intercessor.[1]

A compassionate and mighty intercessor. What reassuring words! I leaned forward to kiss a Byzantine icon of St. Nicholas which stood before the saint's tomb. As my lips touched the painted wood, a subtly-sweet fragrance arose and the perception of a nearby presence grew even stronger. I glanced about, but saw no one in the dimly lit crypt. Still, the sense of being with an invisible and miraculous "someone" was overpowering.

My heart began to feel warm, as though it were getting a big hug without my outer self even being touched. I recalled this sensation dimly as a childhood experience associated with warmest memories of trust. Suddenly, I knew—absolutely—that a living person who was also a saint in heaven loved me!

At that moment I received my gift . . . finding the hope and faith which had been lost so long ago.

And at last I knew the St. Nicholas Secret!

∽A Holy Embrace

7

The Secret Revealed

Ironically, I regained my belief in St. Nicholas just as my children were on the verge of losing theirs. John's misgivings were growing. One night after my return he put his face into his pillow and began to weep.

"What is wrong, son?" I asked, stroking him.

At first he could not answer. But after a few moments he

exclaimed, "I don't know if St. Nicholas really puts presents under the Christmas tree!"

So the long-dreaded moment had arrived at last. John's faith in Christmas morning treats was weakening. And of course it had to—eventually children must know the truth.

"But why are you asking this?"

"Because there are presents for children but none for grown-ups," John continued tearfully. "Why doesn't St. Nicholas bring presents for grown-ups?"

"That is easy to answer. There are no presents for grown-ups because adults should already believe in St. Nicholas."

"What? I thought presents were for being good," Lily protested. "The song says: 'He knows when you've been bad or good, so be good for goodness' sake.' "

"Well, good behavior is important, but that is not the reason St. Nicholas blesses us with gifts," I insisted.

"Besides, I've never heard of anyone who didn't get toys from St. Nicholas, even if they weren't nice," added John.

"Right, because the purpose of the gifts should not be to reward children, but to help them remember heaven. The gifts are just a little sweetness here on earth to remind us of the true sweetness we will find later with God."

"Presents are to remind us of heaven?" John asked.

"Yes. Some people have a very sad time at Christmas being busy and thinking only of this world. They get no joy from either giving or receiving presents because they have forgotten heaven."

"Why does St. Nicholas give presents just to children?" Lily asked.

"So children will love and believe in him. When children believe in St. Nicholas, it is easy for them to believe in heaven, for he lives in heaven. And when children believe in heaven, it is easy for them to believe in our God who created heaven."

John's face was lined with anxiety. "But does St. Nicholas really put the presents under the Christmas tree?"

"Your parents put them there in St. Nicholas' name," I said gently. "But we do this to help you learn about something you can't see with your eyes—to help you believe in something which is not of this world, but is still very real. A miracle is something which is in this world but not of this world—a bit of heaven on earth. And that's what St. Nicholas is."

"But Papa," John said hesitantly, "is there really a St. Nicholas?" Fear and hope filled his countenance, a petitioning dread which I remembered well. He wanted to believe, but needed help.

"How could there not be?" I asked. "I have met him. Not only that, he showed me his secret!"

Pandemonium erupted at this statement, a clear demonstration that, to children at least, material gifts are not the essence of Christmas. John, Lily, and Victoria jumped and hooted as though springs had been released in their limbs, and it was several moments before we could continue.

"Papa, tell us his secret!" they begged breathlessly, with eyes like stars.

The Secret Revealed

"Well, it is simple really," I said. "St. Nicholas' secret is just that he is no fable for children to outgrow. He is a real person living in heaven who can be part of our lives, not only when we are very young, but always. He showed me that it is good for children to think about Santa Claus or whatever they may call him, provided that their small faith in this cheery fellow grows to big faith in God's heaven." (And he also showed me that parents have a very important job in this. They must help children—not let their faith stumble over North Pole elves or flying reindeer.)

"St. Nicholas is real!" Lily squealed happily, while her big brother grinned from ear to ear. I sighed with relief. These children had learned who really sets out Christmas presents while retaining their faith in the One who inspires those actions. They had received a new truth without sacrificing an old hope. They had transferred their affections from childhood's sweet myth to a dynamic reality who could bless all their future years.

Icon of St. Nicholas

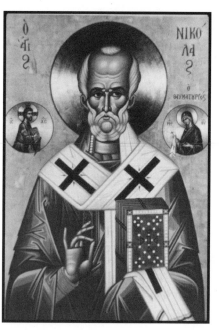

The Saint Nicholas Secret ❧

Suggestions for Parents

Few things so fill children's hearts with wonder and joy as the prospect of St. Nicholas secretly bringing them personal gifts on Christmas Eve. The perception of the love, benevolence, wisdom, spirituality, and power manifested by this ancient personality, together with his seemingly superhuman abilities, fosters one of youth's most memorable dramas.

Wonder can engender and deepen faith, for the Holy Scriptures link it directly to God. Acts 3:10 tells us that the people of

Jerusalem "were filled with wonder and amazement at what had happened" when they saw the lame man whom Peter had healed in the name of Jesus Christ. St. Nicholas, who also called on Christ's name, has in turn become an ageless wonder to generations upon generations—many of whom may celebrate his perennial generosity without comprehending its spiritual foundation.

The rapturous awe and delicate faith of children is precious and should be protected from this world's stodgy materiality and unbelief. Their innocent trust in St. Nicholas must not be allowed to run afoul of the market-based commerciality rampant during Christmas. Parents and other interested adults ought to seek out opportunities to bridge the gaps between huckster and holiness.

This may be accomplished by teaching children early on about

The Saint Nicholas Secret ✞

the real St. Nicholas. They should be familiarized with his earthly life, filled as it was with benevolent deeds guided by Christian principles. They should come to understand that he is not dead and gone, but alive and accessible in heaven. The gradual process by which St. Nicholas came to be known as "Santa Claus" (a corruption of the Dutch version of Saint Nicholas, "Sinter Klaus") should be explained so that the fantasy legend of the latter receives less and less emphasis, while the historical and heavenly reality of the former receives more and more.

Why is St. Nicholas so closely associated with Christmas? Perhaps because he loved to give, as did the Magi who brought gifts to Baby Jesus, and because he had a special love for children. Or perhaps simply because he was so devoted to Jesus Christ. Most likely, it is because his feast day of December 6 falls within the scope of what the world knows as the "Christmas season." (In the Orthodox Church, the time from November 15 to December 24 is a penitential, anticipatory season known as Advent or Christmas Lent. The true Christmas season, the time for rejoicing in Christ's birth, runs for twelve days *beginning* December 25.)

December 6 is the date on which, sixteen hundred years ago, St. Nicholas died to this earthly life and was born into heaven. In many cultures children set their shoes before the door at bedtime on the eve of December 6. The next morning they may find small treats of fruit and candy inside which are meant to remind them of St. Nicholas' love. Reviving this tradition in our homes may help children to separate St. Nicholas from "Santa Claus" in their minds.

One of the best things parents can do is to help children form their own relationship with St. Nicholas. This can be done effectively and easily through prayers to the saint in which children participate. Having an icon of St. Nicholas is useful in providing a reverence-inspiring image of this loving person—one devoid of cartoonlike characteristics. Lighting a candle before the icon helps to focus attention and create a reverent atmosphere. Assure children that St. Nicholas hears them, and that the bond they form with him while still young can outlast all childhood fancies.

For parents whose own education has not prepared them to understand the intercession of saints, it may be helpful to recall the words of Holy Scripture: "Therefore we also, since we are surrounded by so great a cloud of witnesses, let us lay aside every weight, and

the sin which so easily ensnares us" (Hebrews 12:1). St. Paul's reference to a cloud of witnesses has been understood since earliest times to refer to the Church Triumphant, that is, those Christians who have already gained their heavenly victory. In heaven they are neither out of sight nor out of mind, but rather they constantly surround and support the Church Militant—that is, all Christians still on earth working out their salvation.

As Christ has conquered death, so those who belong to Him live forever. Should we be surprised if saints' concerns and prayers for fellow Christians continue even after they have entered a higher realm? It would be a strange anticlimax if all that awaited those who have "fought the good fight," as St. Paul calls it, were an eternity of peacefully doing nothing in particular. Fortunately, the vast evidence of intercessory activities on the part of Christian saints offers convincing assurance to the contrary. The life hereafter will not be characterized by dull lounging about in golden mansions, still less by floating on clouds while playing harps, but rather by an even more intense continuation of that good service to others which so pleases God. (For more on this subject, see the booklet, "Prayer and the Departed Saints," published by Conciliar Press.)

The interaction of saints with living Christians is therefore normal and divinely ordained, especially among those who have a particular calling in this regard. St. Nicholas is one such, who by many miracles has demonstrated his ongoing love for humanity. For the past fifteen hundred years his relics have produced a miraculous substance, Holy Myrrh, in confirmation of his particular ministry

to mankind. The many documented healings and blessings attributed to this saint provide confident grounds for believing that he both hears and answers prayers. His evident love for children is far more than a cozy folk tale—it is an ageless truth which should be imparted to all young souls craving the deeper knowledge of God's salvation.

Epilogue

The manifestation of God's power called Holy Myrrh has not been limited to St. Nicholas of Myra. Other saints' relics have exhibited this phenomenon, for example St. Dimitrios, patron saint of Thessalonica, Greece, and St. Nilus of Mt. Athos, Greece. Of St. Dimitrios it is recorded, "Christians secretly took his body and gave it burial, and there flowed from it a healing myrrh by which many of the sick were healed."[2]

St. Nilus was called "the Myrrh-streaming" due to the copious amounts of Holy Myrrh his body produced. *The Prologue from Ochrid* reports, "When he entered into rest, myrrh flowed from his body in such abundance that it ran from the top of the hill right down to the sea."[3] St. Nilus' seventeenth-century lifetime places him well within the scope of recent history, and the reader can take comfort in the knowledge that all these occurrences have been thoroughly documented by multiple reliable, objective observers over a substantial length of time.

In May of 1953, St. Nicholas' tomb in Bari was forcibly opened in connection with restoration work on the church. Antonios Markou reports:

> A commission was set up for this purpose by the Pope, with Enrico Nicodemo, the then Roman Catholic

Archbishop of Bari, as its president, and was entrusted with giving canonical recognition to the Relics in the tomb. Parallel to this, the inspection, or reconnaissance, and the measuring of the bones was entrusted to Luigi Martino, the Professor of Anatomy at the University of Bari, and to Dr. Alfredo Ruggieri, his assistant.

The sacred Relics were found in a monolithic reliquary of hard rock. Since the period of their deposition in 1089 the reliquary had been covered with a succession of stone slabs. The Relics in the reliquary were floating in a transparent, colorless and odorless liquid, which was almost 300 centimeters deep. The

examination of the liquid by the Institute of Chemistry and Hygienics at the University of Bari showed that it was clear water, "free from salt and devoid of microorganisms." The inquiry proved that this liquid came from the marrow of the spongy bones.

This fact constitutes the scientific confirmation of the myrrh-gushing of St. Nicholas' relics. . . . Texts of the 11th and 12th centuries attest that when the Barian sailors broke into the Saint's reliquary in Myra, they found his sacred Relics in a "divine liquid or oil" *(sanctus liquor-oleum)*. Moreover, the continuation of this extraordinary miracle even in Bari is demonstrated . . . by the existence of four apertures—in the reliquary and in the three slabs which cover it—from which, with the aid of cotton wool or cloth, it was possible to extract the myrrh, which even today has the name "mana" *(manna)*.[4]

St. Nicholas is one of the world's most popular saints. His fourth-century lifetime predates all the later schisms of the Church, so he truly belongs to all Christendom. Since his generous nature serves as a reminder of God's gift of His own Son to mankind, his story has come to be associated with Christmas and passed from culture to culture. St. Nicholas is said to be more frequently represented by artists and to have more churches dedicated to his memory than any saint except the Virgin Mary.

St. Nicholas' significance can be deduced from noting the eleventh-century conflict surrounding possession of his bones. Seamen from Bari sailed to Myra in Asia Minor and bore the saint's relics by force back to Italy. This "translation," as it is called, occurred in 1087, and St. Nicholas' crypt remains in Bari to the present day. The record of this event is captured in a twelfth-century Greek manuscript entitled, "Narration of the recovery of the relics of our holy Father and Wonderworker NICHOLAS."

> When Alexius was Emperor, and the foreign and infidel hordes that had migrated through the Roman Empire were being pacified, and the bold Normans who had voyaged thither had been beaten

and dispersed, certain citizens of the city of Bari, moved by a divine inspiration, purposed to sail in their ships to Myra and remove the fragrant remains of our blessed and inspired Father [Nicholas]. Disembarking at Myra, these mariners found monks watching beside the holy grave of the Blessed, and requested them to make known to them where the saint's body lay. The monks, thinking that they had made the request in order to reverence the body, answered, "Be assured that this is the sacred and venerable tomb of the Blessed from which the sacred oil wells up."

The men of Bari forced their way into the

miraculous tomb, at which the watchers rent their garments and pulled their hair and beards, bewailing their misfortune piteously. And one of them whose name was Lupus, a priest holding a glass vial filled with the prelate's sacred oils, when he saw that his comrades were in distress, let it fall from his hands and heard it crash upon the stones, and he and his companions turned toward the vial and discovered it to be intact. Wherefore they offered fitting praises to God and to His servant and acknowledged with full accord that the will of God and of the saint acquiesced in the removal of his remains from there. For the visitors now had full assurance that the saint was escorting them, and saying: "Here is the tomb in which I lie; take me then, and depart; for the people of Bari are to be forever protected by my intercession."

And a monk answered: "If it has been granted to you to remove the venerable remains of the saint, go on your way in peace, with all good-will and resignation from us. For we shall stand condemned, if we do not obey the injunctions of our holy Father. But we trust, God willing, that he will not allow us, his servants, to remain entirely bereft."

Then one of the men of Bari, taking up a huge mallet, hammered with great force at the cover of the

floor, which was over the oil-exuding tomb, and straightway shattered it. And digging into the hole, led on by the welling favor of the sacred oil, they discovered a splendid chest. And when they had opened it they saw the glory of God, for they found it filled with sacred oil. Immediately such an odor was wafted up to them that they seemed to be standing in Paradise. And not to them alone was the odor vouchsafed, but it pervaded even to the harbor to those in the ships.

Then one of the men, Matthew, descended into the sacred and holy tomb, and dipping his hands into the sacred oil, he beheld the venerable remains glowing like coals of fire. Then the men assembled and, together with the priest bearing the sacred remains on his shoulders, repaired to their ships, praising the ineffable providence and benevolence and power of God. When those who were in the boats heard the great force of their hymn which they were singing to Christ the Saviour, with inexpressible joy they received their fellow sailors, adding their own praise to theirs.

Meanwhile, the inhabitants of the city learned of all that had happened from the monks. Therefore they proceeded to the wharves, all of them heavy with affliction. And they wept for themselves and their

children, that they had been bereft of so great a blessing. And lamenting, they cast themselves into the sea, taking hold of the rudders and oars of the ships. Then with wailing and groans they said, "Give us our patron and our champion, who protected us from our enemies visible and invisible, who has been with us for so long a time, from the time of the great, Christ-loving Emperor Constantine."

While they were making lament the men of Bari answered most kindly, saying, "Realize, brothers, that we are Christians, and that the saint appeared to us in a vision and bade us disembark here and carry away his venerable remains. And brethren, why do you stand frustrated and desolate over him? Behold, as you yourselves have said, many generations have passed under the protection of the saint, and you and your fathers have possessed his healings and blessings. But now his will is to give light to the western world, departing from hence."

The men of Bari placed the venerable and holy remains of our blessed and inspired Father in a very small wooden chest. Then at sunset, when a favorable breeze had arisen, upon a calm sea they set forth on their long voyage. When they were at sea a little gull came and perched upon the venerable remains, and giving forth its lyric song, it caressed

them tenderly. And when they had come to the city [Bari] harbor, they were welcomed joyously by the townsmen and their fellow citizens. The folk, running from the four corners of the city, gathered in his church, suffering from various sicknesses. And there were cured that night and the following morning forty-seven men, women and children. Very many others who enjoyed bodily integrity, received conversion and salvation of soul.[5]

Endnotes

1. *Offices of the Orthodox Church: Saint Nicholas the Wonderworker,* translation from the original Greek made at the Orthodox Monastery of the Veil of Our Lady, Bussy-en-Othe, France.
2. Bishop Nikolai Velimirovic, *The Prologue from Ochrid,* Lazarica Press, Birmingham, 1986, p. 113.
3. Op. cit., p. 189.
4. Antonios Markou, *Concerning the Relics of St. Nicholas of Myra,* translated from the Greek by Patrick G. Barker, Center for Traditionalist Orthodox Studies, Etna, California, 1994, p. 18.
5. *The Translation of St. Nicholas,* translated from the original Greek by McGinley and Musurillo, S.J., Bollettino di S. Nicola, Bari, 1980.

About the Author

Dennis E. Engleman is an author, photographer, and electrical engineer who lives near Atlanta, Georgia, with his wife Deborah, and their three children. His book *Ultimate Things: An Orthodox Perspective on the End Times,* was published by Conciliar Press in 1995. He writes regularly on a variety of Orthodox subjects, and his numerous articles have been published in various magazines.

Also Available from Conciliar Press

Ultimate Things: An Orthodox Perspective on the End Times
by Dennis E. Engleman:
Presents a thoroughly Orthodox, non sensationalistic perspective on the End Times. Thought provoking and well researched.

A Faith Fulfilled
by Michael Harper:
Well known leader in the evangelical and charismatic movements of the 70's and 80' tells of his spiritual journey from Anglicanism to the shores of the ancient Orthodox Church.

Aloysha's Apple
by Alvin Alexsi Currier and illustrated by Nadja Glazunova:
Delightful folk tale from Old Russia. Told in poetic text and colorful illustrations in the classic fairy tale tradition Aloysha's Apple tells a story of the triumph of courage, faith, and love.

From Darkness to Light
by Sister Anne Field:
The early Fathers of the Church—theologians such as Chrysostom, Augustine, Ambrose, and others—speak about the true meaning of Christian baptism and the Eucharist, the Lord's Prayer, Christian life, and other timeless topics.

Call (800) 967-7377 to request a free catalog of other books, booklets, brochures, and gift items produced by Conciliar Press.